T0004865

The Day Hope Was Born
God's Gift of Love
Second Edition

The Day Hope Was Born
God's Gift of Love
Second Edition

By: Sandra Lott

TATE PUBLISHING
AND ENTERPRISES, LLC

The Day Hope Was Born: God's Gift of Love
Copyright © 2014 by Sandra Lott. All rights reserved.

No part of this publication may be reproduced, stored in a retrieval system or transmitted in any way by any means, electronic, mechanical, photocopy, recording or otherwise without the prior permission of the author except as provided by USA copyright law.

The opinions expressed by the author are not necessarily those of Tate Publishing, LLC.

Published by Tate Publishing & Enterprises, LLC
127 E. Trade Center Terrace | Mustang, Oklahoma 73064 USA
1.888.361.9473 | www.tatepublishing.com

Tate Publishing is committed to excellence in the publishing industry. The company reflects the philosophy established by the founders, based on Psalm 68:11,
"The Lord gave the word and great was the company of those who published it."

Book design copyright © 2014 by Tate Publishing, LLC. All rights reserved.

Published in the United States of America

ISBN: 978-1-62746-543-4
1. Religion/ Christian Ministry/ General
2. Religion / Christian Ministry / Evangelism
14.09.24

Contents

INTRODUCTION

In a world where there is sickness, diseases that take lives, families falling apart, unemployment rising and prices along with it, nations fighting against nations and innocent citizens reaping the consequences—people need hope. People need hope that there is something better and that there is something more to this world, well, there is and His name is Jesus Christ. Jesus is everything we need. He is our Master, our Lord, King of Kings, our Prince of Peace, Lion of the tribe of Judah, our Messiah, Immanuel, Wonderful Counselor, Strongtower, A Friend that sticks closer than a brother, Mighty God, Everlasting Father, Lamb of God our Savior. The love of God does not compare to anything else in all creation nor can anything separate us from it. **(Romans 8:35-39)** "Who shall separate us from the love of Christ? Shall trouble or hardship or persecution or famine or nakedness or danger or sword? As it is written: 'For your sake we face death all day long; we are considered a sheep to be slaughtered.' No, in all these things we are more than conquerors through Him who loved us. For I am convinced that neither death nor life, neither angels nor demons, neither the present nor the future, nor any powers, neither height nor depth, nor anything else in all creation will be able to separate us from the love of God that is in Christ Jesus our Lord." Nothing else can fill us the way He does, love us the way He loves us or save us. His names say it all.

Jehovah-Self-existent, I Am that I Am--whatever we need is who He is.
Elohim-Strong one.--He is all powerful. No one or nothing is mightier!

Adonai--Lord- He is God, Lord and He should be Lord over everything
El Elyon--Most High God
El Olam--Everlasting God
El Shaddai--Almighty God
El Roi--The Strong One
Yahweh--I am the One; Isarael's Covenant God
Jehovah Jireh--The Lord Provides
Jehovah Nissi--The Lord is my Banner
Jehovah Shalom--The Lord is Peace
Jehovah Raah/Rohi--The Lord is my Shepherd
Jehovah Rophe--The Lord Heals
Jehovah Shammah--The Lord who is Present
Jehovah Tsidkenu--The Lord our Righteousness
Jehovah Mekadesh--The Lord your Sanctifier
Jehovah Sabbaoth--The Lord of Hosts
Jehovah El Gmolah--The Lord God of Recompense
Jehovah Nakeh--The Lord who Smites
Jehovah Ezer--The Lord our Helper

Our God is Omniscient, Omnipresent and Omnipotent meaning all-knowing, everywhere and all-powerful. Jesus is the only way to the Father and to an eternal home in heaven. **(John 14:6)** "I am the way, the truth and the life. No one comes to the Father except through Me."

Jesus is everything we need and He is our hope, **(Ephesians 1:11-12)** "In Him we were also chosen, having been predestined according to the plan of Him who works out everything in conformity with the purpose of His will, in order that we, who were the first to hope in Christ, might be for the praise of His glory." He is Almighty, powerful and more loving than any of us can really comprehend! He wants to care for us as we do for our children! Praise God, for He truly is amazing! **(Psalm 68:19)** "Praise be to the Lord, to God our Savior, who daily bears our burdens." The hope we have in our hearts given to us through Jesus Christ will help us to believe and trust in God and an eternal home with Him. **(I Peter 1:21)** "Through Him you believe in God, who raised Him from the dead and glorified Him, and so your faith and hope are in God."

Hope and faith in Jesus is not only for the knowing that life does continue once we leave here, it is also for the life we are living today. As you read above, there are many different names for Jesus, this tells you that whatever you need, that is what He is, "I Am that I Am." He will give you hope that will fill your heart with peace giving you strength to continue on to deliverance. **(Romans 15:13)** "May the God of hope fill you with all joy and peace as you trust in Him, so that you may overflow with hope by the power of the Holy Spirit." He will give you hope for every circumstance, every trial and the assurance that He will guide you through it and lead you through to victory. **(Psalm 60:12)** "With God we will gain the victory, and He will trample down our enemies."

When Christmas seasons come and go, remember the true meaning of Christmas, it is the time when Love and hope was born. God sent His love into the world to save us and give us hope for an eternal life with Him. **(John 3:16-18)** "For God so loved the world that He gave His One and Only Son, that whoever believes in Him shall not perish but have eternal life. For God did not send His Son into the world to condemn the world but to save the world through Him. Whoever believes in Him is not condemned, but whoever does not believe stands condemned already because He has not believed in the name of God's One and Only Son." But our Almighty Father in heaven does not want anyone to perish**. (I Thessalonians 5:9-10)** "For God did not appoint us to suffer wrath but to receive salvation through our Lord Jesus Christ. He died for us so that, whether we are awake or asleep, we may live together with Him." Calvary was all about a love and forgiveness so great, that it brings salvation, an eternity in heaven with God our Father to all who believe. **(Romans 10:13)** "Everyone who calls on the name of the Lord will be saved." Through the death of Jesus Christ, upon believing in Him and receiving Him, we have eternal life. **(Acts 4:12)** "Salvation is found in no one else, for there is no other name under heaven given to men by which we must be saved."

Do you need the light and love of God in your heart? Let the short stories and poems in this book help give you a clearer picture of the love of God and receive Jesus, the light of the world into your heart. Your heart will light up with His eternal light, dispelling all darkness and His joy will overwhelm you! **(II Corinthians 4:6)** "For God, who said, 'Let light shine out of darkness,' made His light shine in our hearts to give us the light of the knowledge of the glory of God in the face of Christ."

A CHRISTMAS MIRACLE

Is there a miracle in store for you? Just take a look around
and see the beauty of the world. It's there for all to see.
There are trees big and small and flowers of every color.
There are mountains standing high; some are rocky with a
beauty all their own and some are covered with a diversity of
trees, with leaves of different sizes and just as beautiful when
blowing in the breeze. There are springs of water
everywhere, some flow into rivers, some into lakes and still
others into the sea which flows into the oceans wide and
deep.

 Is there a miracle in store for you? The beauty of the world
in which God created is a miracle in itself. But if that is not
enough; take a breath. The air that you breathe and the
ability to breathe in itself is a miracle from God. Look into
the eyes of a newborn baby and you will see the miracle of
birth and life in which God has given to you and me.

Is there a miracle in store for you? From the creation of the
world to the breath of life given to each of us, God gives a
miracle every day.

Yet, He gave us another miracle in the birth of Jesus Christ.
The miracle He gave us in Him is the gift of eternal life.
This gift is for free and it is for all who will believe and
receive. This is the greatest miracle of all!

THE DAY HOPE WAS BORN

Mary walked out of the doctor's office and just stood there a moment. The sky was blue, the sun was shining brightly and there wasn't a cloud in the sky. She smiled as she listened to the birds chirping in the trees in the park across the street. It was such a beautiful day and after all, she did have the rest of the day off—so she decided to walk across the street to the park and enjoy the beautiful day. Mary sat on a bench underneath a big oak tree. She didn't realize, but she had a smile that radiated a look of wonder and pure joy on her face. Denise, another patient from the same doctor's office sure noticed as she sat down beside her.

Denise had just received some bad news; her test results were in and the doctor said that the cancer had spread. He gave her 6 to 8 months at the most. She had been receiving radiation treatments on and off for the past few years and just could not beat the cancer. It look like it won and she felt as if the wind had just been knocked out of her. She knew she would have to face it one day but until today it never seemed real. Denise knew Mary had been receiving the same treatments and wondered how she could look so peaceful and full of joy. Denise just did not understand; how could she be so happy? It really bothered her so she had to ask.

The two women just sat there a while before Denise finally spoke up, "I saw you at the doctor's office today; how did your visit go?" Mary, taking her eyes off the birds in the tree that seemed to have captured her thoughts said, "About the same. I have to keep going through radiation but the outlook does not look good. He is going to take some more tests next week. I had a mastectomy last year and it looks like it is back and has spread. I guess I will know one way or another in the next week or two if before long I will be making my journey home soon."

Denise, still in a lot of confusion asked, "Home, what do you mean and how can you look so happy and peaceful after receiving news like that? The doctor just told me that I have less than a year to live. My heart is shattered and I don't know what I am supposed to do now."

Mary looked at her and smiled. "My true home is in heaven. We are all here temporarily. Life is preparation for eternity in heaven. Don't you believe in that?" Denise looked at her with tears in her eyes and said, "No I don't. My parents always told me that life evolved and when we die that is it. I can't imagine being here and living one day and then gone the next."

Mary looked at Denise with a soft look of compassion and gently hugged her. She looked at her and asked "tell me which of these has the better outlook. There are 2 boys and one parent told the 1st boy that if he got good grades all year long they would go on a vacation in the summer. They would go to a place where there would be swimming, boating and fishing, all the things he loved to do. The other boy's parents told him that he needed to get good grades, period end of story with no exceptions and he would be in trouble if he didn't get them. The school year passed by and the 2nd boy struggled all year long with the pressure that was on him. He looked worried and not as happy as he used to be, he couldn't wait for the year to get over with and in the end he made 2 D's. The 1st boy went through the year, studied hard and there were a few times when he had a rough time and thought he would fail but he was not worried. He enjoyed the teachers he had this year; school actually seemed kind of fun and at the end of the year he made A's and B's. Which boy went through the year easier due to the hope of a wonderful summer to look forward to?" Denise looked back at her and said, "that is easy, the 1st boy." Mary said, "You are right. That is what hope does for you. You have something to look forward to and it gives you strength and encouragement to make it through even the most difficult times. When you have hope you are happier and a lot more peaceful. So, looking back at this story which boy would you rather be?" "The first one," Denise said.

Mary asked her, "Have you ever heard of Jesus?" Denise embarrassingly looked at Mary and said, "I have heard a little here and there but whenever I asked my parents about Him they always told me it was nonsense. They said I had to be logical and there was no way possible that anything I may have heard about Jesus was true." Mary asked her, "Since the outlook that you have right now from the doctor's report is very grim at best and in knowing what hope does for you, do you want to hear about Him now? Do you want to believe? Isn't better to have something to look forward to then to have nothing at all? Isn't it better to believe that death is just traveling through a door from one life to another rather than thinking you are hear one day and gone the next? Even if I am not right, I have hope, joy and peace instead of sadness; which one would you rather have? Denise sat there a moment. There was a long pause between them as she dwelled on everything Mary had just told her. Mary made sense and she did always seem to be happy every time she saw her at the doctor's office. With that in mind she looked back at Mary and said, "I want to believe."

Mary told her to sit back and listen to a story, a story about the day Hope was born. Long, long ago just as a watch has to have a creator, a watchmaker, it just does not all of a sudden appear, God created the world. God is spirit, He is love and truth. There is no flesh in Him. He wanted someone to love; just like all of us. So, He created man. Knowing that we are flesh and the flesh is weak, it causes us to be tempted, so God gave man laws to follow. Although,

He knew we would never be able to follow them. Just like the 2nd boy in the story. Having rules to follow puts pressure on you and under pressure, most people do fall. The laws were only put in place to show us that we needed Him; after all everyone wants to be needed. He had a plan all along; but God is a God of covenant and there were consequences to breaking the law, consequences that would keep us from Him. He did not want that because the reason He created us in the first place was to be with Him in eternity as one family forever and ever; to be with Him in heaven. Heaven is a place where there is no sadness or death or sickness or evil, only love. God is love. The sin and evil of mankind grew but God being love, still loved us and wanted us with Him. Most people will only love when loved back. God loved us when He created us and He loves even when we sin against Him. Love cannot deny itself.

God knew He had to put His plan into action or all of mankind would end up in hell and away from Him. Since the flesh is weak and "all fall short of the glory of God" He knew He would have to work out salvation Himself. In order to take on the sentence of death that the law brought and to understand the weaknesses of the flesh God knew He had to come down in the form of a man, but He still had to be God so here is where Mary the Virgin Mother of God comes in; as told in the Old Testament from the line of David comes a Savior. The Holy Spirit visited Mary who was from the line of David and she became pregnant with Jesus. She had not been with Joseph in any way yet; so the birth of Jesus was strictly by the power of the Holy Spirit. This way Jesus was all man and all God.

It was time for her to give birth and there was no room for her at the inn so Joseph made a bed for her and the baby Jesus in a nearby manger. The stars were out in the sky and the animals were all around. Even the animals knew. An angel appeared to some shepherds keeping watch over their flocks nearby and told them of the Messiah that was about to be born. 3 kings far away even heard of His birth and they took off at once to see this awesome sight. A bright shining star led them directly to Him. They brought Him gifts of gold, incense and myrrh. The gold represents His deity and the incense and myrrh represent the sweet smelling aroma of our love and praises. The moment was there and Jesus was born. There was a bright light shining all around Him. He radiated the love and the glory of God. All who saw Him knew that this was indeed the Son of God. That night Hope and Love was born. Hope that life does not end here on earth, hope for a Savior, hope for when no one else is there to love you, help you and give you victory over every situation God is there to do just that and His love never ends. Over 2000 years ago Hope and Love was born to mankind. God came to earth to save us. Jesus suffered at the hand of mankind and was hung on a cross and died and was buried. All by the mankind He came to save. He knew we would do that to Him and did it anyway. He rose on the third day and ascended into heaven, but He left His Holy Spirit with us to dwell in all who will receive Him. His Spirit gives us His love, hope, peace, joy, strength and ability to endure all situations. All who believe in Him, receive Him as Lord and ask Him into their heart have this same hope and are given the right to be children of God.

(**John 1:12**) "Yet to all who received Him, to those who believed in His name, He gave the right to become children of God."

Mankind needed a Savior and looked in all the wrong places. God wants our love and He wants us to be with Him. He wants it freely; He does not manipulate. The Bible tells of God and His love, it tells of who God is; it is His story. Satan lies, tempts and deceives. Satan came to earth to destroy Gods beloved creation. So when Satan came down to destroy us, Jesus came down to save us. He promises us that we will live with Him in eternity forever.

(John 3:16-17) "For God so loved the world that He gave His one and only Son, that whoever believes in Him shall not perish but have eternal life. For God did not send His Son into the world to condemn the world, but to save the world through Him."

God knew that in order for us to have His love and joy He needed to give it to us to live within us through His Holy Spirit.

(Romans 15:13) "May the God of hope fill you with all joy and peace as you trust in Him, so that you may overflow with hope by the power of the Holy Spirit."

(Galatians 2:19-20) "For through the law I died to the law so that I might live for God. I have been crucified with Christ and I no longer live, but Christ lives in me."

Since God is Spirit, through Jesus born into the world and after His resurrection we were able to receive His Spirit. All you have to do is believe and ask for forgiveness. We "all fall short of the glory of God," since we are flesh and the flesh is weak and in the light of a Holy God not one of us could live up to the conditions of the law. So, we all sin; you must believe in His unselfish act of love, ask for forgiveness and receive Him; ask Him into your heart. Ask, yes you must ask, for He is "gentle and humble in heart," He will not force Himself on anyone which is why it is said, **(John 1:12)** "Yet to all **who received Him**, to those who believed in His name, He gave the right to become children of God." In asking and receiving you can have the same hope that I have; the hope of going home.

(I Peter 1:3-5) "Praise be to the God and Father of our Lord Jesus Christ! In His great mercy He has given us new birth into a living hope through the resurrection of Jesus

Christ from the dead, and into an inheritance that can never perish, spoil or fade—kept in heaven for you, who through faith are shielded by God's power until the coming of the salvation that is ready to be revealed in the last time."

Denise had been listening so intently with tears rolling down her face. She wiped the tears from her cheeks and said, "You make it seem so clear. Especially after explaining what it really means to have hope. It is like I won't really be dying, but moving to a new home, a better one. Tell me again how I can have this hope, how I can have this promise of a new home. Tell me how to be saved?

Mary reached over with overwhelming joy at the prospect of having a new sister in Christ and hugged her! She told her,

(Romans 10:9-10) "That if you confess with your mouth, "Jesus is Lord," and believe in your heart that God raised Him from the dead, you will be saved. For it is with your heart that you believe and are justified, and it is with your mouth that you confess and are saved."

Denise prayed with Mary and the light of God's love and joy filled her heart and her face. She glowed with the love of God. She finally understood the peace that Mary had because she had it too. She also had the same hope. Today Hope was born in Denise's heart. She may have only 6-8 months here on earth but she now knew she had an eternity in heaven to look forward too.

REDEEMING EYES OF LOVE

I have walked the road of heartache and pain and gave my heart away somewhere along the way.

The roads I've traveled since are many, some were bitterness and anger, some were self-pity and others unforgiveness. In giving it away numbness filled my heart.

Yet through all the clutter and walls that I myself erected round my heart, YOU still loved and saw me with Your **Redeeming Eyes of Love**.

You placed an angel on my path that saw right through my self-made walls. She looked at me with Your Redeeming Eyes of Love and led me straight to YOU.

I let YOU in and gave my heart to YOU; though I thought my heart was lost, YOU had it all along. I hold the key to let YOU in and YOU hold the key to make it new again.

My story is not over; a new path I needed to begin with roads paved with love and restoration created for me before time began.

Each road is hard and involves a process of tearing down my self-made walls. With each step I take and each road I walk a wall comes tumbling down.

Now, instead of walls around my heart the tree of life grows there. My heart was never lost to YOU and the love in YOUR **Redeeming Eyes** has replaced the heartache and pain with joy and fullness of life!

HI, MY NAME IS JESUS

Marie lay silently in her bed as she wiped the tears from her eyes once again. She cried herself to sleep quite often; the pain in her heart was just too overwhelming to keep inside and it seemed as if it wanted to come out more and more. Marie had suffered a lot of heartache in the last 15 years and it had taken a toll on her heart. She was more messed up inside than even she knew. Her marriage had been rocky for several reasons. Marie loved her husband with all her heart; even today she still does. She, through her own sins had received Jesus as Lord; she knew she couldn't do this life thing without Him; but she had to reap the consequences of her actions before she found Jesus and she knew that quite well. She had separated from her husband and met someone else. This was wrong but out of desperation to be loved, she shoved that thought right out of her mind. But it caught up to her and played apart along with her husband's mess, in hurting their marriage and their family. This was part of her heartache and some of it was due to the long road of addiction that her husband has been bound to; this changed him so much and he did not even see it. His addiction to alcohol and drugs kept him angry and short patient. He made Marie feel as if life was about him and making him happy; she felt as if she wasn't human enough to deserve to have wants and needs and desires of her own. She hurt so much inside. Now it is over, but she wasn't about to give up on her husband. Jesus did not give up on her, so how could she give up on her husband or her marriage. All Marie could feel was a deep sadness. She had lost almost everyone that truly loved her and she felt as if she had no one. Marie had 2 sons that were 2 years apart. The youngest at 16 years old was killed in an automobile accident. She let him take the keys the night he was killed; he was on his way to pick his dad up from a country bar and on the rough dirt road they lived on he lost control of the car. It was more than she could bear. That shattered her heart even more and brought up a lot of pain in her oldest son's heart. He had a lot of depression that he could not get past and his life has been a mess; due to his own heartache, he had not matured emotionally or spiritually. Then to add to that she lost both of her parents each to a different illness. Marie always knew she could count on them; she knew her parents loved her. Now, she felt all alone and nothing in her life seemed to be going right; she felt as if she was bound in a prison cell with no key to let her out. She hurt so much inside and was desperate to have someone love her. She loved the Lord but with everything going wrong in her life she didn't think He wanted to bless her and she didn't feel like she deserved it. She felt totally rejected by everyone, including Jesus. Her mind knew better, but her heart just couldn't accept it; everyone had either hurt her or left her and this caused her not to trust anyone.

Marie had lost her job and decided to move back home to Texas where her sister and two brothers lived; she needed to be around her own family again; she needed to be around people she knew loved her. She found a church to go to and really liked it; the people there truly seemed to have the love of Christ in them and made her feel welcomed and appreciated. This did not make the pain go away; it still visited her every night. She had had enough and cried out to the Lord, "Jesus you have to do something! I cannot live like this anymore! I feel so trapped inside my pain and don't know how to get out!" Some friends that went to the same church had told her where she needed to go and who could heal her and they took her to meet Him. They took her to meet her Father.

Marie was so excited! At last she was going to be healed! She came up to the door and it was very hard to open. She wanted to come inside so very much but she just couldn't turn the handle. She talked with some of her Father's friends, but not Him. She went home that night hurting worse than she did before she came. Marie cried herself to sleep once again. Her hopes had been so high; she just knew she was going to meet her Father and He would make all her pain and sadness go away. It hurt so much; the pain in her heart was too much to bear.

A week had past and she thought about the things her Father's friends had told her. They said He loved her and that His love was inside her heart; it was there from the very moment she believed in and received His Son. She just needed to believe it for herself.

It was Monday and she was going once again to see her Father; this time she didn't know what to expect. Her Father's friends led her in and talked to her for a while. They had been visiting with Him and they knew why she couldn't open the door the first time she came. Every door has a key and when the right key is put into the door it unlocks making entry easy and without any work. She had not used the right key. They went on to tell her she was of royal blood; a princess; a daughter of the King. She needed to believe this and receive it into her heart.

She said it and finally as the words came out of her mouth they seemed to go inside her heart at the same time! She believed it! Finally, she did believe in her heritage! She had said it before, but through all the pain and heartache in her life she did not think she was worthy of being a daughter of the King of Kings. But now she did believe; she finally believed! Now, as she turned the handle, the door opened! Yet, as hopeful and excited as she was, she still had trouble making it to the Father. Marie went home; this time she had hope as if for the very first time. Her Father's friends had told her that she had so much pain inside it would take time, like peeling off the layers of an onion.

The next evening as she settled in for the night, she felt a tugging at her heart. She knew what she needed to do. Marie decided she was going to see her Father all by herself. She came to the door and it opened; she walked down the hall very slowly. She still seemed to have a little fear; but only a small amount now and she was not going to let that stop her. Even in her determination her legs seemed almost paralyzed as she continued down the hall. She kept saying to herself as she walked, "My Father loves me and I am a daughter of the King." Each time she said it she moved closer and closer. She walked down the hall repeating the same words over and over. Finally, she could see someone up ahead. He was holding His arms out to her. She could barely look at Him; His eyes like doves looked like pure love. He held out His arms to her and said, "I love you and what I did—I did for you too!"

Marie couldn't seem to make her feet walk any faster and felt as if she was 5 years old. The more she repeated the words, "My Father loves me and I am a daughter of the King," the easier it was to draw close to the Man who held out His arms. Oh, how she wanted Him to hold her! Finally, she made it; she stood there in front of Him and said, "I believe and I do accept your gift! I know you died for me too!" With that, she threw her arms around Him and He held her tight as He said, "Hi, My name is Jesus, welcome home!"

A cooling rain of her Father's love filled her heart and surrounded it. She finally saw her Father, she saw Him through the Eyes of Love as she gazed upon the wonder of Jesus all snug in His arms. The pain had vanished and Marie finally felt and knew down deep in her heart that **she was loved and she was home.**

In accepting Jesus for who He was and believing that He and His Father loved her completely her heart felt complete and whole. Her Father's door was not hard to unlock after all; she had the wrong key the first time. She went in fear, fear of being rejected. They right key to open her Father's door is to believe in Jesus and to receive Him into your heart. For, "without faith it is impossible to please God."

You see, Marie's Father is God and the only access to Him is by faith in Jesus; faith not works. You cannot do enough good deeds in your whole lifetime to gain access into His house; that is why the "tower of Babel" did not work. If you could it would be by your merits giving you the glory instead of the One who suffered and gave His life you. There is nothing you can do own your own to gain access; no one comes to the Father but by Jesus Christ.

(John 3:16) "For God so loved the world that He gave His One and Only Son, that whoever believes in Him shall not perish but have eternal life."

I DIED TODAY

Lifeless in Your hands, You carry me.
I am dead to the world and to my flesh
that You may live free in me.

I have fought and wrestled against the struggles
in my heart, wanting all the pain to be free from me.

The answers to my pain You already knew.
There was only one thing that I needed to do.

Yet I struggled on, trying in my own way and
praying in desperation. The fight continued on;
my heart truly broken. I cry out, "Please God,
show me Your way!"

You knew the way and were patient
with my stubborn heart; fighting for
it's own way and failing to see it Yours.

Weary from the pain and the trials that wore
me out; I fall lifeless into Your hands. The path
has broke my heart.

I finally died today. My will inside me gone.
It's buried with my pain and in Your hands I lay.

My heart cries out, "I'm tired Lord, there's no
more fight, my heart struggles no more."

To my amazement, the peace I sought finally
came. When to my will I died and I called to

You and gave myself. My heart will never be the same.

That was the way all along. For God is great
and His way is best. We must die to self and seek
His grace; in us let His glory be revealed that we
may see His face.

He'll wait patiently to hear us say, "Lord, not my will,
but Thy will be done." His peace will come and you
will never be the same. When in your heart His
presence known, you will shine; His glory known
in Jesus name.

THE HEART OF WORSHIP

Mary had come to a crossroads in her life; it seemed as if every road she had taken up until now had led to destruction. She was on a downward spiral and knew she needed a change. Mary felt empty inside and did not know how to fill that emptiness. Love was a big part of it but she searched for it in all the wrong places. She had searched for it in the arms of a different man every month and the temporary peace that came from the drugs and alcohol they brought. Nothing worked but she did not know of any other way; that is the lifestyle she learned from her parents. Mary's dad, for as much as she could remember of him spent his nights at a neighborhood bar and when he was home, all her parents did was fight. Then, one night he went out as usual to the bar and never came home. Mary was only nine years old and although she did not like to hear her parents fighting, she still loved her father and needed his love. She felt abandoned by her father; and thought he should have loved her enough to stay. Her mother sank into her own little world after that, which surprised Mary. As much as her parents fought she thought her mother would be relieved, but that was just not so. Her mother seemed to go through the motions of life after that and she drifted from one job to another and one man to another. There was no time for Mary in her mother's life. She was now abandoned by her father and her mother. Her mother was still there but her heart was somewhere else. As Mary grew, the desperate need to be loved drew her in the wrong direction. Mary threw herself into school activities at first and was very good at everything she did, she needed to be accepted. Although she excelled at first in school, it did not seem to fill the void in her heart. Then in high school she met a boy named Roger with a bad boy image and was immediately drawn to him. It was not the image that drew her as she later discovered. It was her need to be loved by her father and he reminded her very much of him. Roger was bad news right from the start, he was into drugs, hanging out on the streets at night and doing anything and everything to get money for alcohol and drugs. The more Mary hung out with him the more her grades dropped and the more withdrawn from the world she became. She kept searching but not even the love of Roger filled that void. Soon Mary was doing drugs as well. She left school and home and moved in with Roger. He lived in an apartment that was roach infested and in a part of town that even the police department did not even like driving through. It wasn't long before Roger started prostituting Mary just so he could get drug money. Mary felt worse now then ever before and nothing, not even the drugs she lived on made her feel better. Mary felt abandoned and unloved and unwanted by her parents. She felt rejected and to add to that she hated and was ashamed of herself for all the men she slept with; she had lost her self-respect and any ray of hope that she may have once had of ever really being loved. It wasn't long until Roger had been shot in a gang shoot out and Mary was left alone again. She left home, quit school and now the only person that she relied on was gone, even if the emotions Roger had for her was merely for his own self satisfaction, he was there and all she had. Mary had no where to go, no money and was about to be kicked out of the apartment she lived in, dingy as it was, it was still a place to lay her head. She walked the streets with no where to go and no plans of any kind. She walked out of inner city, without a particular direction in mind, she just started walking. About a mile from a Church called Faith, Hope & Love Church of God, Mary went into an alley by a nearby store to find a place to sleep. Her face was dirty and her clothes looked as if they had not been washed in weeks. Her hair looked like she didn't know a brush even existed. All she could think of was to find a place to sleep. She had no home, no job, no money and no one to love her. All her hope was gone. She found a huge crate that was laid out on its side by the grocery store garbage can and crawled up inside and went to sleep. She slept all evening and all night.

Pastor Joseph McKinley was taking his morning walk; he loved to walk through the neighborhood. It was his chance to see the glory of God's creation, walk and talk with Him and be His hands and feet as well. He loved being a Pastor, but he loved even more reaching out to the world outside the Church. He always said, "the sheep inside are drawing from the Master's care and are being fed, but it is the ones outside that need our love, help, hands and hope for they are ripe for the wolf to attack who is always close at hand." Pastor Joe would not have seen her at all if her foot had not have been sticking out, but it was more than that, as he walked by a dove flew right by him barely missing his nose and perched right on top of the crate. It drew his eyes right to her. He knew God was directing him to her for "His eyes are always on the sparrow." **(Job 36:15)** "But those who suffer He delivers in their suffering; He speaks to them in their affliction." Pastor Joe walked up to her and as gently and as quietly as he could he touched her and asked, "Miss, do you need some help?" She woke up with fear in her eyes and said, "Excuse me?" Pastor said again, "Do you need some help? My wife and I live a short distance away and if you are hungry and need a place to sleep you are very welcome to come with me." Mary was as about as far down as she could get, so being prideful right now would not do her any good. Too ashamed of herself to look him in the eye she quietly said, "Yes, I would surely love something to eat." Pastor told her to come along and even said that he had a teenage daughter with some clothes that would fit her if she wanted to take a shower. The moment he said that, a sparkle of light gleamed in her eyes; Mary couldn't remember the last time she had a shower! As they neared the house, Mary quietly asked, "Mister, will this be ok with your wife?" Pastor Joe reassured her that his wife was gentle and loving and welcomed new visitors to their house as much as he did. Mary did not know he was a Pastor yet and Pastor Joe did not think it wise to tell her just yet. He thought it might scare her away and he knew by the look of hopelessness in her eyes that she needed his help.

Pastor Joe's wife was just as he said she was and his children, a seventeen year old daughter Angela and his fourteen year old son, Matthew was just as warm hearted and welcoming. Mary had never known this before; it made her feel uncomfortable and at the same time she liked it. She just did not know how to handle the sincere love that seemed to shine from all of them. She only knew the kind that had to be paid for either with her body or doing her chores as a child, (which was the only thing that made her parents notice her at all). Mary had taken a shower and put on the set of clothes that Angela had given her and already Mary was beginning to feel as if she was coming back to life from a very long sleep. Pastor Joe's wife, Ruth gestured to Mary to come into the kitchen. In a sweet gentle voice Ruth told her, "Mary, my husband and I talked and we would like to offer you a place to stay for as long as you need one. We would love to have you here with us." Mary did not know what to think. No one had ever shown her such kindness. Everyone always wanted something in return and this had truly caught her by surprise. She had no other options and did not relish sleeping on the street again; so she accepted their offer. The next day Pastor Joe went to the church to work on his sermon for Sunday and Ruth was in the kitchen cleaning up the breakfast dishes when Mary walked in, seeing Pastor Joe leave she asked, "Where is Mr. McKinley going," (that is how she knew him). Ruth told her that he was the neighborhood Pastor and was going to the church to work on his sermon. Mary was somewhat startled by this news, she did not know what he did for a living yet. She had seen churches but really did not know what they were all about; her parents had never taken her. Very quietly and almost embarrassed to ask, Mary spoke up and asked, "What is a church Miss Ruth?" Ruth sat down next to her and smiled and told her that it was where people go to worship and to learn about the Lord. Again Mary felt embarrassed, but wasn't as scared to ask this time because Miss Ruth did not make her feel stupid for asking, instead when she answered her question there was a gentleness in her voice that made her feel calm and welcome. She quietly asked, "Who is the Lord, I have seen churches but my parents never took me to one?" They sat there for hours as Ruth explained about God, the Father who created the world. She told her that the world did not pop into existence, like a watch that has to have a watchmaker; the world had to have a Creator. This seemed to make sense to Mary and she nodded her head as to tell her to go on. Ruth went on to explain that as every child growing up needs discipline from their parents and to teach them right from wrong, God does the same with us. She explained that every action has a consequence here on earth but it also makes a difference as to where we spend eternity when we die. She told her "to be absent from the body is to be present with the Lord," that we all have spirits breathed into us by our heavenly Father and when we die as long as we have made Jesus our Lord and Savior, our spirits will go up to be with Him in heaven where we will live for eternity. Mary always wondered what happened when a person dies and listened intently. But she still did not know who Jesus is and asked, "I sort of understand the dying part, but who is Jesus?" Ruth told her about the first people God had created and how bad the world had started to get, the sinful ways in which people were living. She went on to tell her about the Ten Commandments and in obeying God you are blessed, but in disobeying, as with your own parents you are punished. She went on to tell her about Satan and how God had to cast him from heaven and how Hell would be his eternal dwelling place. Ruth also told her that "he roams the earth seeking whom he may devour." Mary asked her, "Miss Ruth, if God is so powerful, how come He just doesn't make people do right." Miss Ruth excused herself for a moment and came back with a toy robot that belonged to her son. She told her to look at this robot and how he is made to do only certain things and cannot do anything unless he is programmed to do it. She asked Mary, is there any real life in the robot? Mary said, "No." Miss Ruth went on to tell her that God wants His children to love Him freely, so He gave us free will. He will direct and lead and heal but it is our choice whether we listen and obey. If He took free will away, He would have to take all of it away and then the love He wants from us would not be offered up freely and would not mean as much. She asked Mary, "Do you want people to love you because you make them, or because they want to? Mary told her that she wanted it to be because they want to, but she had never known that kind of love, at least not until now. Ruth told her that man is made of flesh and the flesh being weak, it always wants its own way and that usually disagrees with God's ways. It is only through being a child of God through atonement that you have His Holy Spirit which enables you to love God, love people and obey God. The sin of mankind needed to be paid for, but if God left that to each of us, "For all have sinned and fall short of the glory of God," no one would end up in heaven with God. The very reason He created us was to be His children." **(John 1:12)** "Yet to all who received Him, to those who believe in His name, He

31

gave the right to become children of God." "This verse is talking about is Jesus, God's one and only Son. You see Mary, God knew all along that mankind could not live up to His holy standards and there had to be atonement for our sins. He had a plan all along. So, He sent Jesus, His one and only Son to be that atonement." **(John 3:16-18)** "For God so loved the world that He gave His One and Only Son, that whoever believes in Him shall not perish but have eternal life. For God did not send His Son into the world to condemn the world but to save the world through Him. Whoever believes in Him is not condemned, but whoever does not believe stands condemned already because He has not believed in the name of God's One and Only Son." "Jesus came to earth and taught the people how to live and how to love one another. He healed all their diseases, made the lame walk and even brought some back to life. And some, the Pharisees who had a lot of high standing among the people and loved the power and recognition it brought them, knowing there was something special about Him, but did not want to accept the identity of who Jesus was, denied it. They had Him put to death. They hung Him on a cross; He died and gave up His Spirit willingly. It was God's plan all along; Jesus was the sinless Son of God which qualified Him to take upon Himself the punishment of mankind. As He gave up His Spirit, He made it available for us, to help us to love one another as God loves us for "God is love." **(John 14:15-17)** "If you love Me, you will obey what I command. And I will ask the Father, and He will give you another Counselor to be with you forever--the Spirit of truth. The world cannot accept Him, because it neither sees Him nor knows Him, for He lives with you and will be in you." **(John 16:13)** "But when He, the Spirit of truth comes, He will guide you into all truth. He will not speak on His own; He will speak only what He hears, and He will tell you what is yet to come." Jesus did that for us. **(John 15:12-13)** "My command is this: Love each other as I have loved you. Greater love has no one than this that he lay down his life for his friends." "To receive the Holy Spirit all you have to do is believe in God, believe in Jesus and that He died for your sins and ask for forgiveness and ask Him into your heart." **(Romans 10:9-10)** "That if you confess with your mouth, 'Jesus is Lord,' and believe in your heart that God raised Him from the dead, you will be saved. For it is with your heart that you believe and are justified, and it is with your mouth that you confess and are saved." "You see Mary, when you receive, His Holy Spirit, since it came from God; He comes to live within you making you a new person. Sort of like being born again and you then have His attributes, His ability to love and forgive and show kindness to others." **(II Corinthians 5:17)** "Therefore, if anyone is in Christ, he is a new creation; the old has gone, the new has come!" Mary sat back in her chair and had a look on her face as if a light bulb had just gone off in her head. "That is why you and Mr. Joe are so nice to me! It is real with you. I felt it from the beginning; none of you made me feel dirty or like I was nothing. I could feel the love coming from everything that all of you have done for me. You all are true children of God. It must be real because you not only believe in the way you speak about it, but you have lived it and showed me that love since I have been here. So, what is a Pastor?" Ruth told her that a pastor was someone that as He reads God's Word, the Bible, He also listens to what God wants him to speak to the people about concerning a particular verse in the Bible. He reads it to the people or congregation and preaches a sermon to the people that explains what God has spoken to his heart concerning that verse. He is also a counselor in which people can come to him for advice or just encouragement or prayer. He leads and guides the church in having Bible studies to teach the people a little more in depth then what time allows for on Sunday. He also guides the church in outreach programs to help others in our community and also spread the Word of God and His love that we may be the hands, feet and voice of God. Mary had a look of pure amazement on her face. She said "How can I learn more?" Ruth went to a cabinet in a shelf in the living room and pulled out a Bible and handed it to Mary. She told her that they always keep extras in the house to give as needed and told Mary she could have it. She told her that it is the story of God, mankind and Jesus. It is also a guide to how God wants us to live, but more than that, God spoke the world into existence and His Words in the Bible are just as powerful. They give us hope and encouragement and as we speak them over our life, our lives our transformed by them as well.

They had been talking for 3 hours when Ruth noticed the time and said she had a lot of housework to do and welcomed Mary sit on and read or make herself at home while she cleaned. Mary was so excited to read the Bible because all along she wondered why they were being so nice. Everyone before had an ulterior motive but now she knew it was genuine love and concern for her and she wanted to learn more about this Jesus. Mary had gone to church with them on Sunday and was purely fascinated; she still had questions in her heart and still cried herself to sleep at night. She wondered how Jesus could love her, not even her parents did and she had done so much wrong. One thing Mary could not deny was the love she felt from the McKinley's. They had Jesus in their heart and they showed it to her. Finally one day as Mary and Pastor Joe were talking, Mary told her concerns to him. Pastor smiled and told her the story of his salvation. It was very similar to hers. He was strung out on crack cocaine and a nice old couple took him in and loved him enough to help him kick his addiction and turn his life around. Before he finished, Mary was weeping so hard she could not control it. Ruth came out and sat beside her and held her. Mary did not know she had so much pain, she cried for her parents, and the rejection she felt. She cried for the mess she made of her life by quitting school and getting strung out on drugs as well. She also cried for the shame she felt from sleeping with so many different men. She finally asked, "If I ask this Jesus into my heart, will He make my heart happy? I am so tired of hurting inside and so tired of crying all the time?" Pastor Joe told her that God loves her just as she is and about the dove that flew by and perched itself on the crate she was sleeping in and how it caught his eyes. Right then Mary knew that God loved her too and that He had led Pastor Joe right to her. She asked him if he would pray with her to receive Jesus and he joyfully said yes! He told her that her identity was now in Jesus and that she was now a daughter of the King! "The old is gone and the new has come!" Mary did feel like a new person and the hole in her heart that left her heart feeling void and empty was gone; instead she felt a joy so overwhelming that she could not explain or quite understand it herself. She knew she had a long way to go but she also knew that she would be ok. The McKinley's had enrolled her in school; they said she could stay as long as she needed and she just wasn't ready to find her parents. Mary had dropped out in the middle of her junior year. She had her transcripts transferred and started the new school year off as a junior again. She had a lot to make up; she didn't mind and she had become good friends with Angela, their oldest daughter. They were becoming more and more like sisters with each passing day. Mary was learning more and more about Jesus and still had questions about what it meant to worship. Pastor Joe told her that it is a lifestyle you live, you love God so much that you not only love Him and His Son, Jesus, but you love Him by loving others. He told her that it is also a love that comes from your heart; you love Him so much that you have to express it. Sunday in church the choir was playing "Mary's Alabaster Box" and as they sung, she finally understood. She identified with this song. All of a sudden, all the emotion she had felt for God seemed to explode from within her. The devotion was for how she felt for Him in saving her life from living on the streets and maybe more of the same lifestyle she had lived with Roger. It was for healing her broken heart and for also making her feel like a human being worthy of being loved and not something dirty; the love and gratitude she had for Him came forth like a flood! She cried and danced and sang and was totally lost and in a world of her own. She finally understood not only what worship was but who Jesus is, He is life and truth and love. Mary never grew tired of pouring out her love to God in her daily life. She also became known as the girl with a heart for worship and was a real inspiration for the people of the church. More and more people joined her at the altar on Sunday in worshiping God. Worship isn't an emotional feeling; it is a lifestyle of love for God, but it is also a heart thing. Do you have a heart for worship? He died for you? What do you do for Him?

WHERE HAS ALL THE WORSHIP GONE?

Where is the worship? Where has is gone?
The world promotes drinking and drugs and the latest Harry Potter Book in the now. It promotes witchcraft in which You are against. You parted the Red Sea and healed the blind and the sick. Where is Your praise? Where has it gone?

People talk about who did what to whom and that seems to be ok, but talk about my Savior, the One who died for me, and something's wrong with me. I'm just another fanatic. Why is that so? Where is Your worship?

A crown of thorns dug into Your head and nails pierced Your feet. You took our pain and our punishment. You died for us. Where has Your worship gone?

People sit around on Sunday's and watch the latest football game, but go to the house of God; they don't have time for that. You gave Your life, but that is not important enough. Where has all Your worship gone?

Blood ran down Your face, nails pierced your feet.
You died for us. Where has all Your worship gone?

The world does us wrong in some way every day. Do we leave it? Someone in church, human that they are, does us wrong and we leave it. The house of God! Your house where we go to worship You and not the people who go there! Where has Your worship gone?

You carried the cross and was beaten and whipped beyond human recognition. Where has Your worship gone?

There's violence, killing and stealing overflowing in the world and watching desperate housewives seems to be the latest craze. Where is Your worship?

You shed tears for us. You sweat drops of blood before hanging on the cross. You were beaten, laughed at and spit on. A whip marred Your back. Your body was covered in blood. You hung on the cross. You took our pain. You died for us. Where is the gratitude for what You did? Where has all the worship gone? Where is the glory, honor and praise due Your holy name?

CALVARY'S SON

Love is very special between a Father and a Son.
One day they're together and the next
One is Calvary's Son.

A Son given to the world for sins of the heart that
the world could not begin to repent of from all the sin.

He is very special right from the start, and if
you receive Him, you will know the love
that is in His heart.

Do not be a fool and let a day go by, and
miss out on that special love because of fear or pride.

To each life must come and end, and the time
you do not know when. So do not waste that
special love and sit and wonder why, instead of
that special love you cared more about your pride.

Each life is very special, don't wait another moment
to receive the grace from His love and miss out on the
freedom that comes from Calvary's Son.

Your soul is at stake, so don't make a mistake and wait. It
will burn endlessly, with Satan, for an eternity.

So look to Calvary's Son
He'll break the yoke of Satan
and free you from his chains.

Love is very special between a Father and a Son.

It's all about forgiveness and the faith that comes.
When you receive His love.

Don't wait another minute
ask for forgiveness and receive
Calvary's Son.

TEARS FROM HEAVEN

There are tears flowing from my eyes from all the
pain I have inside. My heart can't help but cry.

I love My children so much that I gave them My Son.
He shed His blood and gave His life because the price
was just too much for them to pay. Their debt was just
too high.

So He came and with His blood, He paid the price
and now their debt shows paid!

So, why do I cry? Just take a look around and you
will see. Do they honor Me for wiping their slate clean?
I gave My Son and all I ask is just 2 things. To love My
Son and receive His gift of unselfish love.

But the world and the pain it always ends up
causing seems to draw My children away from
Me and turn down the gift that I offer for free.

That is why the tears keep flowing and My heart keeps
crying. All I want is for them to love Me so I can set them
free. But they keep rejecting Me. The hate and addictions
of the world seem so enticing but come with a high price to
pay. Either with a heart turned cold or their health gone
bad or a life they didn't really mean to take. What a high
price to pay for a heartache they don't even want. When I
can set them free.

My tears keep flowing because My gift to them is free.
But they keep rejecting Me.

My gift will give the peace. My gift will give them joy, My gift will make their hearts feel light and free.
They would soar on eagle's wings. My gift would unite all My children an bring them Love & Peace.

But the tears keep flowing. They keep rejecting Me.
But I am very patient. For I want all of them to be
set free. I will keep waiting for just a little while so I can hear their heart sing, Brothers and Sisters are we, bound together in Christ, we are free!
Then they will be with Me for an eternity!

CARRY ME

Carry me when my trials overwhelm me and my load
gets too much to bear. I run to You and seek
Your face; Your love is always there.

I will worship You and seek Your saving grace
I will worship You and always seek Your face.

Surrendered to your love, I'm carried by your grace.
Your strength holds me up; Your love will never fail or
forsake.

Carry me O Lord; I'm surrendered to Your mercy and Your
grace. Carry me O Lord; Your love will hold me up and
the forgiveness through Your blood has given my heart a
new face.

Carry me O Lord through life's hills and valleys, good
times and bad. Carry me O Lord, I'm surrendered to Your
grace. In repentance all my sins are erased. Your glory I
will always seek because I'm surrendered to Your grace.

Carry me O Lord into the heights of the heavens above
and into the depths of Your love. Surrendered to Your will;
I'm carried by Your grace. Your strength holds me up and
Your love will never fail or forsake.

Carry me O Lord, I'm surrendered to Your grace.
I will worship You and always seek Your face.

THE CROSS THAT LEADS TO HEAVEN

When I start to feel all alone, at those times when the people all around are trying to deter me from the goals set before me by God, I remember Jesus.

When my family or people in general insult me for following my beliefs, in trying to obey God's will, and they try to get me to change to their way because they do not like the way I have chosen, I remember Jesus.

I remember how Jesus stood alone and was betrayed and denied. I remember how Jesus was insulted and ridiculed.
I remember how Jesus was beaten beyond human recognition. (reference Isaiah 52:13-14)
I remember how Jesus wore a crown of thorns that caused blood to run down His face.
I remember how Jesus carried the cross to Calvary, a place called Golgotha.

Jesus took the insults, He was the One who was beaten, He wore the crown of thorns and He alone carried the cross. He alone was crucified. Jesus alone took the pain and the punishment. He alone was put to death. He alone did that for us.

I remember Luke 9:23, "If anyone would come after Me, he must deny himself and take up his cross daily and follow Me." Then I ask myself, "How can I complain?" His load was much heavier than mine.

Then I remember that it was Jesus alone who rose in glory! He did that for us, so we might be saved and live with Him in heaven. He did that for us, so we would have peace and joy eternally.

I remember Jesus and His cross that leads to heaven.

ON THE WINGS OF AN EAGLE

When the problems I face are
too much to bear, I know that He cares.
In my weakness, He's my strength.
He lifts me up on the Wings of an Eagle
and on His love my heart feels lighter than air.

On the Wings of an Eagle
we soar through the air,
through the clouds we ride
and now my problems seem so small.
In my weakness, He's my strength
His love will not let me fall.

When I feel overwhelmed
He's the One I run to, the only One I need.
In His strength, I can carry on.
He guides me through life
On the Wings of an Eagle
His love carries me.

GOD'S ABOUNDING GRACE

Grace is the act of God's unending
abounding love for us.

Grace is:
<u>Understanding</u> when we don't deserve it.
<u>Mercy & Compassion</u> when we don't deserve it.

Grace is:
<u>God Supplying</u> all our needs.
and the <u>strength</u> that He gives us when we are weak.

By God's Grace:
We have <u>Joy & Peace</u> in our heart where
pain and sorrow once dwelt.

By God's Grace:
We have <u>Forgiveness</u> of all our sins
when we don't deserve it.

By God's Grace:
We are <u>Victorious</u>!

Grace is:
<u>The showing of God's love</u>;
when we are hurting,
when we doubt Him;
and when we sin against Him.

By God's Grace:
We have <u>eternal life</u>, through Jesus Christ our Lord.
Grace is: Calvary and a love everlasting.

GOD'S GRACE

Your grace is sufficient for me.
I am not always abounding with joy and
My faith seems to take a giant size nosedive.
But there is something that I am always
Aware of and will always declare,
Your grace is sufficient for me.

I sometimes stumble and fall and
Detour from your path
Always at my side; walking beside me
Is where You are; listening for my call.
Your grace is sufficient for me.

When I finally call out Your name
The fear and pain in my heart go away.
The light of Your love opens my eyes
And Your faithfulness I see.
As Your love fills me with joy and peace
Once again, You Word becomes alive in me.
Walking beside me You will always be.
Your grace is sufficient for me.

FINAL THOUGHTS

The purpose of this book was to shed some light and understanding into your heart of the true meaning of God's love and give you something you can share with the people in your life that have not received Jesus as Lord and Savior. Let the Holy Spirit speak to your heart through the poems and the short stories within the pages of this book, the Holy Spirit is the Spirit of Truth and He will give you the understanding to receive it, just ask. (John 16:13) "But when He, the Spirit of truth comes, He will guide you into all truth. He will not speak on His own; He will speak only what He hears, and He will tell you what is yet to come."

Letting go of the desires of your flesh and the hold it has over you which is 'dying' to our sin nature and can only be done through Jesus Christ. He gives you all the strength you need to endure. Through the trials you go through, as you depend on God and spend time with Him in prayer and through reading His Word, you will grow closer to God. You learn the truths and promises that He reveals to you in His Word. That, the spiritual gifts given to you by the Lord, and the fruit of His Spirit helps you to endure and persevere through your trials and to help others in their trials. (Romans 5:2-5) "And we rejoice in the hope of the glory of God. Not only so, but we also rejoice in our sufferings, because we know that suffering produces perseverance; perseverance, character; character, hope. And hope does not disappoint us, because God has poured out His love into our hearts by the Holy Spirit, whom He has given us." Our Heavenly Father sends the Holy Spirit, and the fruit of the Spirit indwells in us, upon receiving Jesus into our hearts. (Galatians 5:22-23) "But the fruit of the Spirit is love, joy, peace, patience, kindness, goodness, faithfulness, gentleness and self-control." This is how in Christ we are a new creation. The fruit of His Spirit within us, and going through our trials, we are changed into who God wants us to be. (Hebrews 10:10) "And by that will, we have been made holy through the sacrifice of the body of Jesus Christ once for all." God did not leave us helpless, He sent Jesus to be everything we need. If you need a love in your heart that will complete you in every way, call on His name and ask Him into your heart, for He lives to intercede. (Hebrews 7:25) "Therefore He is able to save completely those who come to God through Him, because He always lives to intercede for them."

Jesus is God's gift of love and hope to you and with His Holy Spirit dwelling within your heart you will have an eternal peace that will help you to go through any situation. Have you received Him? Read through the scriptures on the next page and pray the prayer at the end. It is that simple and it will eternally change you.

GOD LOVES YOU!

(Jeremiah. 31:3 "I have loved you with an everlasting love; I have drawn you with loving kindness.")

I Timothy 2:3-4 "God our Savior, who wants all men to be saved and to come to the knowledge of the truth."

He will not knock on the door to your heart forever. Will you let Him in?

Revelation 3:20 "Here I am! I stand at the door and knock. If anyone hears My voice and opens the door, I will come in and eat with him, and he with Me."

Jesus is the only way to God.
John 14:6 "I am the way, the truth and the life. No one comes to the Father except through Me."

John 3:3 "I tell you the truth, no one can see the kingdom of God unless he is born again."

And, you must make Him Lord of your life.
Matthew 6:24 "No one can serve two masters."
Matthew 7:21 "Not everyone who says to Me, 'Lord, Lord', will enter the kingdom of heaven, but only he who does the will of My Father who is in heaven."

We must leave our old ways behind.
Mark 3:25 "If a house is divided against itself, that house cannot stand."

You can't live according to the flesh and desires of the sinful nature and expect to have Jesus in your heart. He is holy. He is love. Love and Hate cannot exist together.

Ephesians 4:22-24 "You were taught, with regard to your former way of life, to put off your old self, which is being corrupted by its deceitful desires; to be made new in the attitude of your minds; and to put on the new self, created to be like God in true righteousness and holiness."

God gives you the ability to do His will. He knows it is hard.
Philippians 4:13 "I can do everything through Him who gives me strength."

Romans 3:23 "For all have sinned and fall short of the glory of God."

I John 1:9 "If we confess our sins, He is faithful and just and will forgive us our sins and purify us from all unrighteousness."

John 1:12 "Yet to all who received Him, to those who believed in His name, He gave the right to become children of God."

Romans 10:10 "For it is with your heart that you believe and are justified, and it is with your mouth that you confess and are saved."

Then after you confess and ask forgiveness and receive Jesus into your heart, you must testify (tell someone) and be baptized. In this, God is glorified and others might be saved by your example.

II Timothy 1:8 "So do not be ashamed to testify about our Lord"

I Peter 3:21 "And this water symbolizes baptism that now saves you also-not the removal of dirt from the body but the pledge of a good conscience toward God. It saves you by the resurrection of Jesus Christ."

INVITATION TO SALVATION PRAYER

Dear Almighty Father in heaven, I know that I am a sinner and I ask your forgiveness of all my sins. I want to make You the Lord of my life and I want to serve You all the days of my life. I believe that Jesus Christ died on the cross for my sins. Thank you so much for loving me and waiting on me to come to the knowledge of the truth! Thank you for my salvation. Please help me and guide me in learning your Word so I can be a light to the world. Please, Jesus come into my heart, and baptize me with Your Holy Spirit. I thank You and praise Your Holy Name and ask all this in the Name of Jesus Christ our Lord. Amen.